Kilgore's Catholics

art by
Al Kilgore

created by
Margaret Carroll
&
Jerry McCue

ABOUT COMICS | CAMARILLO, CALIFORNIA

Kilgore's Catholics
originally published as:
   Convent Belles
      published by A. A. Hadinger, 1952
   Saints Alive!
      published by Abbey Books, 1953
   Monsignor
      published by Abbey Books, 1954
About Comics edition published September, 2018

Customized editions available

Send all queries to *questions@aboutcomics.com*

Convent Belles

The Characters
APPEARING IN THIS BOOK

SISTER
BERNADETTE

SISTER
CECILIA

MONSIGNOR
O'MALLEY

MOTHER
ANGELICA

MRS. O'LEARY

FATHER FLYNN

TRUANT OFFICER
CLANCY

ROCCO AND RILEY

BROTHER
AMBROSE

HOBSON

OFFICER
MULLIGAN

O'FLAHERTY

"M-M-M-M-M-M-M"

"I LIKE THIS STORE 'CAUSE IT'S A LONGER RIDE"

"I NEVER DID LIKE BANANAS!"

"I USED TO BACK HOME"

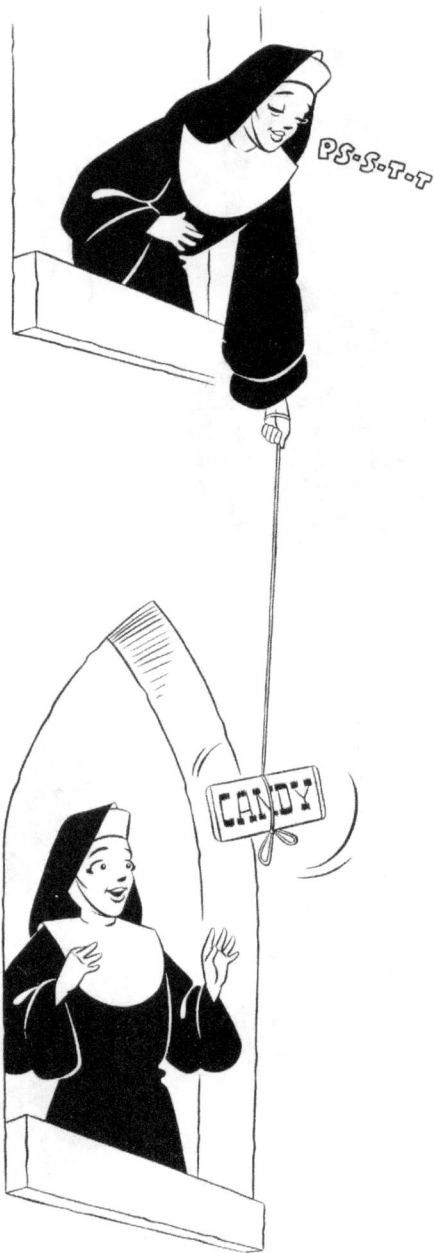

"LET'S, JUST ONCE"

"THIS, I'VE GOT TO SEE!"

"BELIEVE IT OR NOT, PARDNER — WE'RE LOST!"

"WELL, HOW DID HOPPETY MAKE OUT?"

"YOU'RE NEXT"

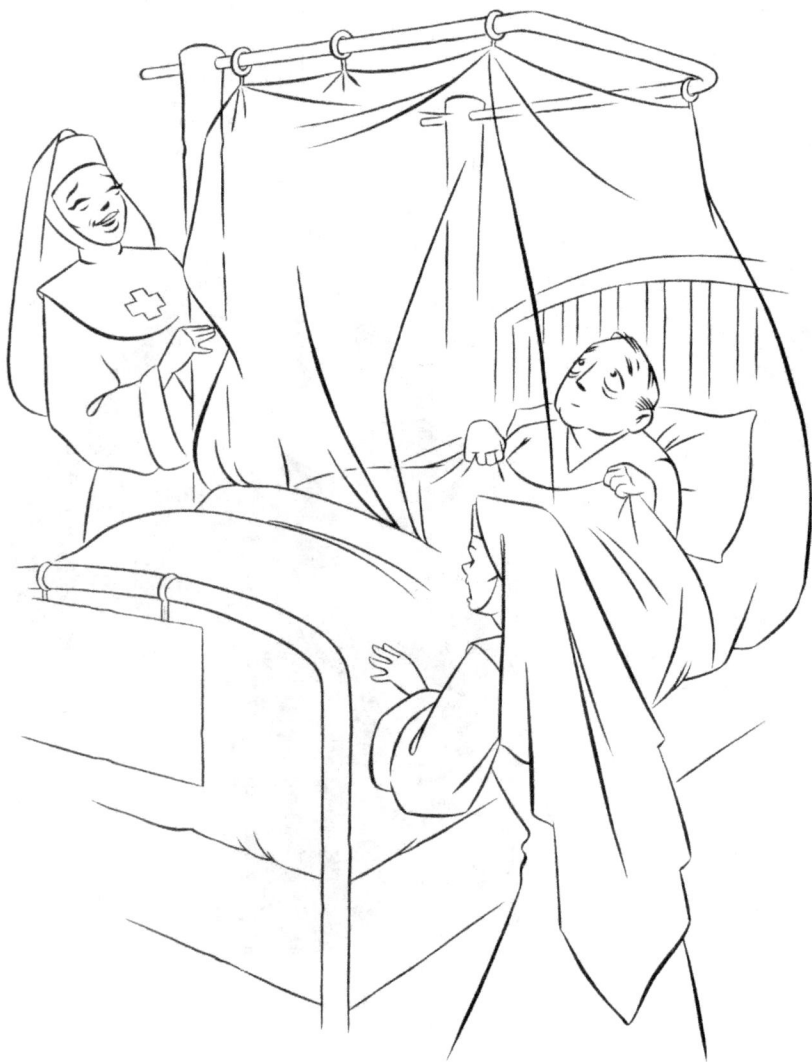

"NOT OXYGEN, SOMEBODY SNUCK HIM AN
ONION SANDWICH!"

° "SOME PEANUTS FOR THE MONKEYS, PLEASE"
° "HOW MAN'A-YOU GOT?"

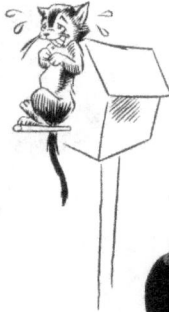

"STEPHEN FOSTER OR NO STEPHEN FOSTER—
THIS HORRIBLE NOISE HAS GOT TO STOP!"

"AH! SPRING IS REALLY HERE"

"O'FLAHERTY HAS COMPANY FOR DINNER"

"MAYBE O'FLAHERTY IS DOWN WITH A COLD,
BUT I REMEMBER LAST ST. PATRICK'S DAY"

"IS IT NECESSARY TO GROW SO MUCH SPINACH?"

"NOW CAN YOU STOP IT?"

"BUT, WHAT'LL WE DO WITH THEM ALL?"

"WONDER WHY IT STOPPED"

"RILEY!"

"YOU DROPPED YOUR SHOULDER - THAT'S
WHY YOU CAUGHT IT!"

• "IF THIS DOESN'T GO OFF, WE'RE STUCK"
• "AND IF IT DOES GO OFF, YOU'RE REALLY STUCK!"

"OKAY EINSTEIN - EVERYTIME ONE OF US GETS OFF, YOU SUBTRACT- GET IT?"

• "STOP WORRYIN' THAT'S ONLY THE FROGS' CROAKIN'"
• "YEAH, BUT IT SOUNDS LIKE CLANCY, THE TRUANT OFFICER, AND IT GIVES ME THE WILLIES!"

"YOU PUSH ME, THEN I'LL PUSH YOU"

"WHADDA YA CALL THAT?"

"PICKIN' VIOLETS — THAT SETTLES IT!"

"WHAT NEXT THROUGH THESE PORTALS?"

"THEY'RE TO KEEP THE SAND OUTA YER
SHOES, — I GUESS!"

"WE BROUGHT THE TOTS IN, LIKE YOU SAID, MR. SPIELHEIMER"

"SHALL WE?"

THE AD-LIB

"THE WALTZ IS ONE-TWO-THREE, ONE-TWO-THREE, LIKE THIS!"

"WHO SAID 3 TEASPOONSFUL TO 1 CUP —
IT'S 1 TEASPOONFUL TO 3 CUPS!!!"

∘ "YOUR PINKY FINGER ISN'T TOUCHING THE KEYS, AT ALL !"
∘ "IT'S SHORTER THAN THE OTHERS, THAT'S WHY!"

"I FOUND SOME YARN UNDER MY DESK"

"THAR SHE BLOWS, SISTER"

WILLIAM TELL • ANTI-CLIMAX

"THEN WE'LL TALK TO THE MANAGER, ALL THESE CHILDREN ARE 7 OR UNDER, AND WE ARE ADULTS, FOR SURE!!"

"NO BRASS RINGS, GOVERNMENT PRIORITY,
SISTER"

"IT WAS FATHER FLYNNS' IDEA TO SHOW US A NEW PLAY"

• "NOW WHO'S GOING TO DIG US OUT?"
• "GUESS WHO?"

"HOW THAT MAN LOVES THAT HORN!"

"IT'S NOT THE ORGAN— SOMEONE'S VOICE
IS CHANGING!"

"DUNKING!"

"WHY, MRS. O'LEARY"

"DUCK! THAT WAS MONSIGNOR!"

"NO TIME LIKE THE PRESENT, MR. MIZEY"

"WELL?"

"WHAT CAN YOU LOSE, MONSIGNOR?"

"DO YOU THINK ANYONE IS LOOKING?"

"WE BETTER CHANGE THE SHAPE – IT MIGHT
OFFEND SOMEONE WE KNOW"

"I HAD HIM IN MY ENGLISH CLASS"

"AIN'T WE LUCKY"

"REMEMBER?"

"DUCKY SPOT, ISN'T IT?"

finis

To
Alfie, Johnny and Kew

o "I HEAR YOUR UNCLE BIM IS SUFFERING FROM
GAS TROUBLE !! "
o "YEAH, HE LIT HIS PIPE IN THE GARAGE !"

"NOW WHAT??"

"SPACE RIDER XB 1-6-2 REPORTING"
"WELL, RIDE BACK TO EARTH FAST, IT'S 9-0-5 A.M."

°"THEY'RE SO IDENTICAL, HOW CAN YOU TELL
   THEM APART?"
°"SIMPLE, ONE IS LEFT HANDED THE OTHER RIGHT,
   WHEN IN DOUBT I JUST THROW A PIECE OF CHALK!"

- "NOW THINK ··· IF YOU HAD 12 APPLES AND YOU TOOK AWAY 9, WHAT WOULD YOU HAVE LEFT?"
- "JUST ENOUGH FOR 3 LITTLE STRUDELS!"

"LA SOCIÉTÉ EST BASÉE SUR UN ÉCHANGE DE SERVICES"

°"MA, WAS ANYBODY FROM SCHOOL HERE
LOOKIN' FER ME?"
°"NO − BUT THERE WAS FOR JOHN RILEY, SR.!"

°"MA, DO YOU MIND IF I BRING HOME SOME
OF MY SCHOOL MATES TO PLAY WITH ME?"
°°"NOT AT ALL, – WHO ARE THEY?"
°"NANCY O'ROURKE!"

"ISN'T YER SCHOOL THAT-A-WAY, GENTLEMEN?"
"YER RIGHT, MR. MULLIGAN, WE HAD SOMETHING
ELSE ON OUR MINDS!!"

"GEORGE WASHINGTON CARVER FOUND MANY
INDUSTRIAL USES FOR OUR AMERICAN PEANUT—
FER INSTANCE — PEANUT BRITTLE, PEANUT CRUNCH,
CHOCOLATE COATED PEANUTS, PEANUT BUTTER
BARS AND SALTED PEANUTS!"

"DON'T LET THAT COLLAR FOOL YOU — HE CAN SURE USE HIS DUKES!!"

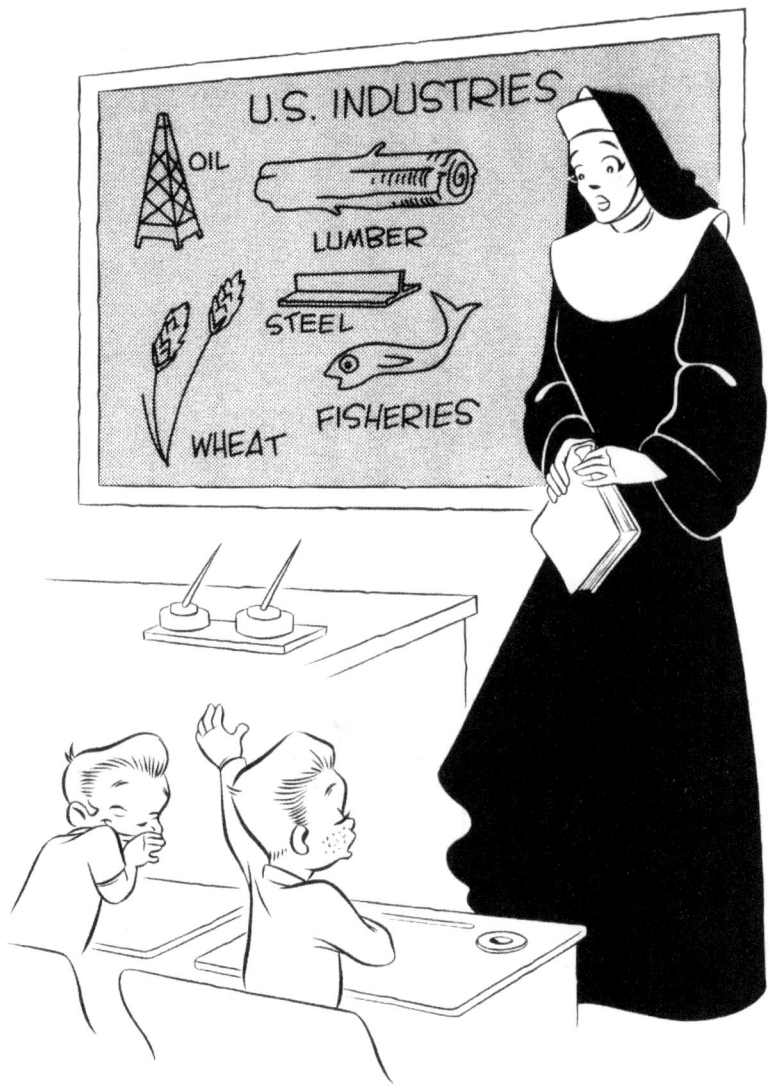

• "... AND WHERE DOES OUR BEST SALMON COME FROM?"
• "THE A & P !!"

"MY UNCLE BIM GOT A PRETTY LIVELY JOB,
AT LAST!"
"YEAH, DOIN' WHAT?"
"CLEANIN' EELS AT THE FISH MARKET!!"

o"CAN YOU UNDERSTAND WHAT LITTLE BROTHER
   IS SAYING, JUNIOR?"
o"YEAH, HE SEZ, 'WHY DO YA WASTE YOUR
   HARD-EARNED DOUGH ON SUCH LOUSY
         STUFF AS SPINACH?'"

"DON'T THEM WHITE AND BLACK KEYS REMIND
YOU OF A LOT OF TEETH WITH CAVITIES IN
THEM, PERFESSER?"

"I'VE BROUGHT THE FIFE AND DRUM CORPS
HOME TO REHEARSE, MA — BUT YOU AND
POP DON'T HAVE TO LISTEN!"

"MAYBE WE COULD USE HIM TO MAKE THE
OPPOSIN' PITCHER SICK!"

"SLIDE, MONSIGNOR, SLIDE!!"

"HERE, HERE, WHAT'S ALL THIS MESS FOR?"
"WE'RE HAVIN' A PET SHOW AT SCHOOL AND WE
DON'T WANT KATHY KELLY'S FANCY POODLE
TO THINK BOZO'S GOT FLEAS!"

"TONY SENT ME!"

.. "HE'S NOT MUCH TO LOOK AT, BUT THEY STAY
   CLEAR OF HIM IN ACTION!"
 . "WHY?"
.. "THEY'RE SCARED OF HIS BITE!!"

"DON'T MIND ME, MONSIGNOR, TODAY'S FRIDAY!"

"NAW YA DON'T, FATHER FLYNN, NO SNITCHIN'
COOKIES FROM THE PANTRY!"

"GLAD TO HAVE YOU JOIN US, BROTHER AMBROSE
NOW WHAT IS IT YOU PARTICULARLY EXCELL IN?"

"WELL, I SHOOT IN THE LOW EIGHTIES AND THAT'S
CONSIDERED PRETTY GOOD GOLF FOR AN AMATEUR!"

° "WHY ARE THE LIMA BEANS SO CLOSE TO THE CORN?"
° "THAT'S THE WAY SUCCOTASH IS GROWN, MOTHER!"

"MOTHER SUPERIOR WAS WONDERING WHY YOU
STOPPED RINGING!"

"LIVER-R-R-R-R"

UMBRELLAS
IN ALL COLORS
WE MATCH
YOUR OUTFIT

"MATCH THIS"

"BUT, IT'S YOUR HUSBAND, MRS. CLANCY, AND HE'S BROUGHT YOU FLOWERS!"

"I'M AMAZED, HE MUST HAVE BEEN TO A WAKE LAST NIGHT!"

"NOTHING SERIOUS FATHER — THE CEILING CAME DOWN ON THE GILHOOLEY'S, UPSTAIRS, AND THEY'RE WAITIN' FER TH' INSURANCE ADJUSTER!"

"NO THANKS, EVERYBODY'S GOT ONE, EXCEPT MONSIGNOR — AND HE CAN'T USE ONE!!"

○ "WE'RE THE COMMITTEE TO SEE MONSIGNOR ABOUT THE PICNIC"

○ "THIS IS NO TIME FOR A PICNIC—FIRST, MONSIGNOR IS
     WORKING ON THE SCHOOL BUDGET AND SECOND, HIS ULCERS
     ARE WORKING ON HIM !!"

"I WAS RIGHT HERE WAITIN' FOR MY MASTER, BUT
WHERE WERE YOU LAST SUNDAY, SINNER ??"

○ "JUST THE GUY I WANTED TO SEE! THE CELLAR
   NEEDS CLEANIN', THE LAWN NEEDS MOWIN', THERE'S
   PLENTY TO DO... THEN I'LL FEED YOU!"
○ "SO, WHOSE HUNGRY?"

"WHY DON'TCHA STOP COMIN' AROUND — YOU
KNOW YOU CHURCH MICE AIN'T GOT NOTHIN'"

∘ "WHAT'S THE SCORE, MISTER?"
∘ "FER YOU AND ME LADS — IT'S THREE STRIKES!"

"LOOK, OFFICER – LET'S NOT STAND HERE AND ARGUE – THERE'S FLOWER POTS UP THERE AND I DON'T TRUST THIS CARTOONIST!!"

° "YES, OF COURSE, THE BED AND MEALS ARE
FREE – ALL WE ASK IS A LITTLE WORK IN RETURN"
° "SOMEBODY GIVE ME A BUM STEER!"

"HAVE YOU FORGOTTEN DR. MULLARKY'S WORDS ABOUT FRUSTRATING A CHILD? — BESIDES YOU CAN ALWAYS BUY NEW PIPES !!"

"PASS IT UP MONSIGNOR, HE PLAYED FIRST BASE AT COLLEGE!!"

"MILD, WITH NO UNPLEASANT AFTERTASTE—**BALONEY**!"

∘ "CAN YOU NAME TWO VERY COMMON FARM ANI-
   MALS AND SOME END PRODUCTS DERIVED FROM
   THEM ?"
∘ "PIGS N' CHICKENS – END PRODUCTS – HAM N' EGGS"

"THIS IS THE TIME CLANCY GOES BY— LET'S HIDE
IN THE TREE"

"CAN I TRY MY LUCK, MA'AM"
"THAT WAY TO THE RING TOSS GAME, ME LAD!"

"CLANCY SURE LOVES THAT TREE!"

"NOW DO YA SEE WHY I OILED THE SPRINGBOARD?"

"- AND THAT MULLIGAN, ME FRIEND, IS **YOUR**
TICKET TO PERDITION— IT HAPPENS TO BE
THE BISHOP'S CAR!"

"BE YE NOT ALARMED, MY BRETHREN, 'TIS BUT
MRS. O'LEARY'S BISCUITS TAKING
ETHEREAL FORM"

"LET'S TAKE A ROW, HUH?"
"WHAT- WITHOUT LIFE PRESERVERS?"

"PSYCHOLOGICALLY SPEAKIN', BROTHER AMBROSE,
WHICH SIGN CARRIES THE MOST SIGNIFICANCE?"

"IF I ONLY HAD THE TIME!!"

°"MONSIGNOR, I HAVE A DRASTIC CONFESSION
TO MAKE, AND I HOPE YOU DON'T MIND!"
°°"GO RIGHT AHEAD, DOCTOR"
°"I THINK I PULLED THE WRONG TOOTH (GULP!)!"

"HOW DOES THE COLOR STRIKE YOU, MONSIGNOR?"

° "I'M GOING TO THAT MISSION IN THE HIGH ALPS!!"
° "FROM WHAT I'VE HEARD OF YOUR SINGING —
   YODELING FOR YOU IS A NATURAL!!!"

"OF COURSE, I REMEMBERED THE BISHOP WAS
COMIN', BUT WITH PRICES SO HIGH—IT HAD TO
BE HASH!!"

"YOU'RE LATE, FATHER FLYNN, YOU MUST'VE HAD A BIG DAY!!"

"SURE DID, THEY TIED THE SCORE IN THE 9TH AND THE GAME WENT 12 INNINGS!!!"

"IN REPLY TO MANY INQUIRIES, THE STRANGE
SOUNDS EMANATING FROM OUR CHURCH,
TUESDAY NIGHTS, ARE FROM OUR CHOIR—
IN REHEARSAL!"

"THERE IS NOTHING SO INVIGORATING AS THE SMELL OF BURNING AUTUMN LEAVES!"

"WADDA YA MEAN, GO BACK FOR HOT TEA?
THIS HAS BEEN STANDARD EQUIPMENT
UP HERE FOR YEARS!!"

°"WELL, I SEE YOU HAD GOOD LUCK, MY BOY,
WHERE DID YOU CATCH THAT EXCELLANT FISH?"
°°"OVER AT GILHOOLEY'S FISH MARKET!"

∘ "ANOTHER "A" TEST??!!"
∘ "NO, PADRE — SMOKE SIGNAL — SQUAW HEAP MAD — SHE SAY, 'COME HOME AT ONCE'"

" YA CAN'T BE TOO SURE !!"

"TRY A SAMBA- AND LET'S SEE WHAT HAPPENS!!"

"CERTAINLY NOT WHILE THEY'RE WORKING
LIKE TWO LITTLE BEAVERS, MR. CLANCY!!"

"AW NO······ IT COULDN'T BE !"

"IT SAYS HERE—'LOCK ALL WINDOWS AND DOORS
SECURELY, LIGHT SULPHUR CANDLE, PLACE IN
CENTER OF FLOOR AND LEAVE THE HOUSE—
GUARANTEED ALL PESTS WILL BE EXTERMINATED'
WELL, ALL WE GOTTA DO NOW IS LIGHT IT AND GO!"

To
Margaret

"WOW! I WISH WE HAD ONE OF THEM SPACE-
SHIPS RIGHT NOW!"

°"OUT OF WORK SINCE LAST XMAS! WHAT CAN
  YOUR LINE BE, ANYWAY??"
°°"PROFESSIONAL SANTA CLAUS!"

"OKAY···· BUT NO LIQUID LUNCH!!"

"DID YOU FIND A BRIEF-CASE WITH SOME PAPERS
  AND BOOKS - - - - - -"

"- - - - - AND SOME PEPPERMINT CANDY? YEAH-
  IT'S DOWN AT THE OFFICE WAITIN' TO BE CLAIMED!"

"UM-M-M- MINCE OR PUNK'IN !"

"I HOPE THAT GUY WENT TO COMMUNION THIS
MORNING!!"

"°-AND THE ANSWER IS **NO**-WE CAN'T AFFORD TO REPLACE THE DEAD GOLDFISH IN THE SCIENCE ROOM!"

°° (MEANIE!!)

"YA CAN'T TOUCH HIM IN HERE – CONSECRATED GROUND, YOU KNOW!"

"SEEMS YOU GOT TROUBLES TOO, EH? WELL, LET'S GO SEE IF WE CAN TALK MRS. O'LEARY OUT OF SOME CHOW!!"

"IMAGINE-- IF OURS BUTTONED THAT WAY!!"

°"FUNNY THING, OYSTERS ON THE HALF-SHELL
DON'T AGREE WITH MY UNCLE BIM!"
°°"TELL HIM HE'S NOT SUPPOSED TO EAT THE SHELLS!"

"I GOT THIS NOTE ASKING ME TO COME HERE—IS IT ABOUT MY BOY?"

"RIGHT—THE KID'S BEEN COMPLAININ'—NOW—YOU LAY OFF OF HIS ELECTRIC TRAINS!!"

"PLANT LESS CABBAGE, O'FLAHERTY, MRS. O'LEARY
SAYS CORNED BEEF IS SKY-HIGH THESE DAYS!"

"... NO WET PAINT SIGN AND
WHAT'S WORSE – YA PAINTED
IT ORANGE!!"

"IT'S TIME FOR YOU TO GET A NEW TAXI, MAGUIRE, UNLESS YOU'RE THINKING OF DONATING TO THE SCHOOL FUND!"

"I CAME FOR A DONATION, NOT EXAMINATION,
NOW DID YOU HEAR?"

3-D

"I HAVEN'T GOT THE NERVE TO TELL HIM TO TAKE OFF THE POLOROID GLASSES!!"

"POKE TH' COKE, WILL YOU?"

"WELL, WHAT'LL YOU HAVE, MR. WISEGUY?"

"SHAME ON YOU - - - - - - PLAYIN' FIREMAN THIS
TIME OF NITE !!"

"MRS. REILLY'S AWAY-BUT YOU'LL FIND THE OLD MAN DOWN THE CELLAR PLAYIN' POKER WITH THE BOYS!!"

"ICE COLD, AIN'T IT?"

"H-M-M — MAYBE A GENIUS, MAYBE A PSYCHOPATH!"

"OKAY, SHORTY- GET IN THERE AND DO YOUR
STUFF!!"

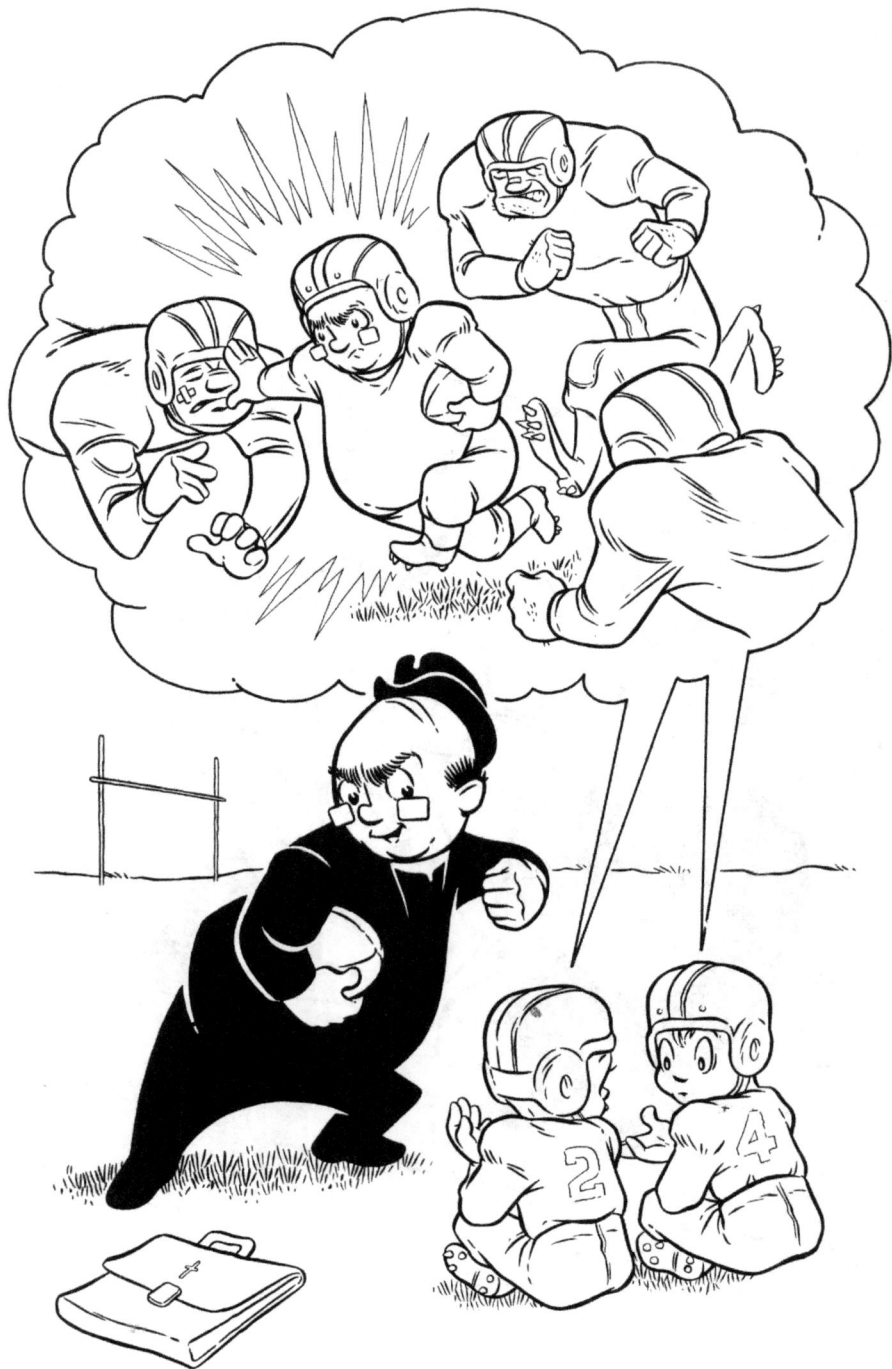

"CURIOUSITY KILLED THE CAT, FATHER!!"

"TELL THE BISHOP I'LL BE DOWN IN A MINUTE!"

"HE'S NOT AS VICIOUS AS ALL THAT --- AFTER ALL, MONSIGNOR, THIS IS THE FIRST TIME HE'S BIT A BISHOP!!"

"COME OUTA THERE, O'FLAHERTY AND GET SOME
SNOW SHOVELED-THIS IS NO TIME FOR HIDE N' SEEK!"

"I NEVER KNEW HE WORE THEM, MRS. O'LEARY!"
"I DUNNO, HE SAYS HE'S GETTING SET FER THE ICE CARNIVAL!!"

"—AND THIS IS THE SAME FIGURE EIGHT IN REVERSE
NOW WATCH HOW I FINISH !!"

°"IF IT'S MONSIGNOR YER LOOKIN' FOR, HE'S OCCUPIED!!"

°°"NO I AIN'T! ... AND GET SOMEBODY TO FIX THAT CHIMNEY DRAFT!!"

"FORGOT TO TELL YOU, MONSIGNOR, THE BRAKES ON THIS JEEP DON'T HOLD SO GOOD!!"

"WHY THE INVENTOR HAD TO SCRAMBLE THESE LETTERS LIKE THIS, I'LL NEVER KNOW!"

"HOW DID YOU KNOW THIS WAS CALLAHAN?"
"I RECOGNIZED HIM BY THAT BLOOD SHOT EYE!!"

"YOU KEEP TELLIN' ME WE NEED A CAR FOR OUR
EMERGENCY CALLS, OKAY, THERE'S ONE WE CAN AFFORD!"
"I'LL SETTLE FOR A BIKE, MONSIGNOR!"

" O, YE SONS OF EVE !! "

"WELL—THERE GOES MY COUGH MEDICINE!!"

"A-A-A-H, SHADDAP!!"

°"AND TODAY I MADE THIS LUSCIOUS DEEP-DISH
APPLE PIE!"
°°"AND TODAY I DESPISE APPLES IN ANY FORM!"

"BUT, MONSIGNOR, WHO'D EVER THINK MURPHY WOULD BE UP THERE?"

"MAYBE YOU TAUGHT PHYSICS --- BUT I THINK
I BETTER CALL THE 'LECTRICIAN, MONSIGNOR!"

"THERE'S NOTHING TO FEAR, WILD ANIMALS
ALWAYS RUN WHEN THEY HEAR YOU COMIN'!"
"YEAH, WHICH WAY, MONSIGNOR??"

"AIN'T HE SUPPOSED TO RUN, MONSIGNOR?"

"THE WORKS, TONY--- BUT BE CAREFUL HOW
MUCH YOU TAKE OFF!!"

"--- JUST MAKE SURE YOU GO TO CONFESSION TOMORROW!"

"HONEST, MONSIGNOR, IT'S WHITE GASOLINE
FER TH' LAWN MOWER!"

"WELL, WHAT ARE **YOU** LAUGHIN' AT ? CAN YOU DO ANY BETTER ?!!"

"IT WAS A HOT-SHOT OFF THE RIM -- DO YOU THINK THEY'LL SEE IT FROM THE FIRST PEW?"

"BROKE MY GLASSES THIS MORNING --- CAN
YOU PLEASE DIRECT ME TO YOUR OPTICAL
DEPARTMENT?"

"I DON'T CARE IF HE DOESN'T LIKE FISH ---
TODAY IS FRIDAY!!"

"MIGHT AS WELL CLOSE UP SHOP WHILE HE'S ON!"

(This page reproduced with the permission of
His Excellency Bishop Fulton J. Sheen)

"AW— WHY DONTCHA GET IN ON TIME LIKE THE REST OF US, MICKEY!?"

"LOOKS LIKE JOE, THE BUTCHER, MADE EARLY MASS!"

"YOU MAY HAVE MEANT THAT AS THE WEDDING MARCH – BUT FROM DOWNSTAIRS IT SOUNDED LIKE 'THE SHRIMP BOATS ARE COMIN'!"

"IF YA LET ME IN WITH IT – I'LL KEEP 'EM AWAKE
FOR YA!!"

"HEY, O'FLAHERTY, CUT IT DOWN LOW SO I CAN
SEE HOME PLATE!!"

"NOW, TELL ME WHY YOU DIDN'T WANT ME TO YANK
THIS UNSIGHTLY VINE OFF THE WALL?"
"TOO LATE, MONSIGNOR, IT'S POISON IVY!"

"DON'T WORRY ABOUT IT, MONSIGNOR, THERE'S NOTHING BREAKABLE IN IT!"

"ADIOS, MONSIGNOR!!"

"I COULDN'T MAKE THE MEETING, MONSIGNOR, BEEN FEELIN' BAD!"

"YEAH, FISH-HOOKS IN YER EARS AIN'T GOOD!!"

"HOTTER'N HELICOPTERS, AIN'T IT?"

"WHATEVER IT IS – MAKE ME ONE EXACTLY LIKE IT!"

" YOU TELL HIM !! "

"SORRY SIR, SHE'S RIGHT! YOU'RE IN THE WRONG BERTH, WRONG CAR — AND WHAT'S WORSE --- WRONG TRAIN!!"

°"WHAT DO YOU RECOMMEND I DO IN CASE OF SEA SICKNESS, DOC?"
°°"THE USUAL THING --- RUN FOR THE RAIL!!"

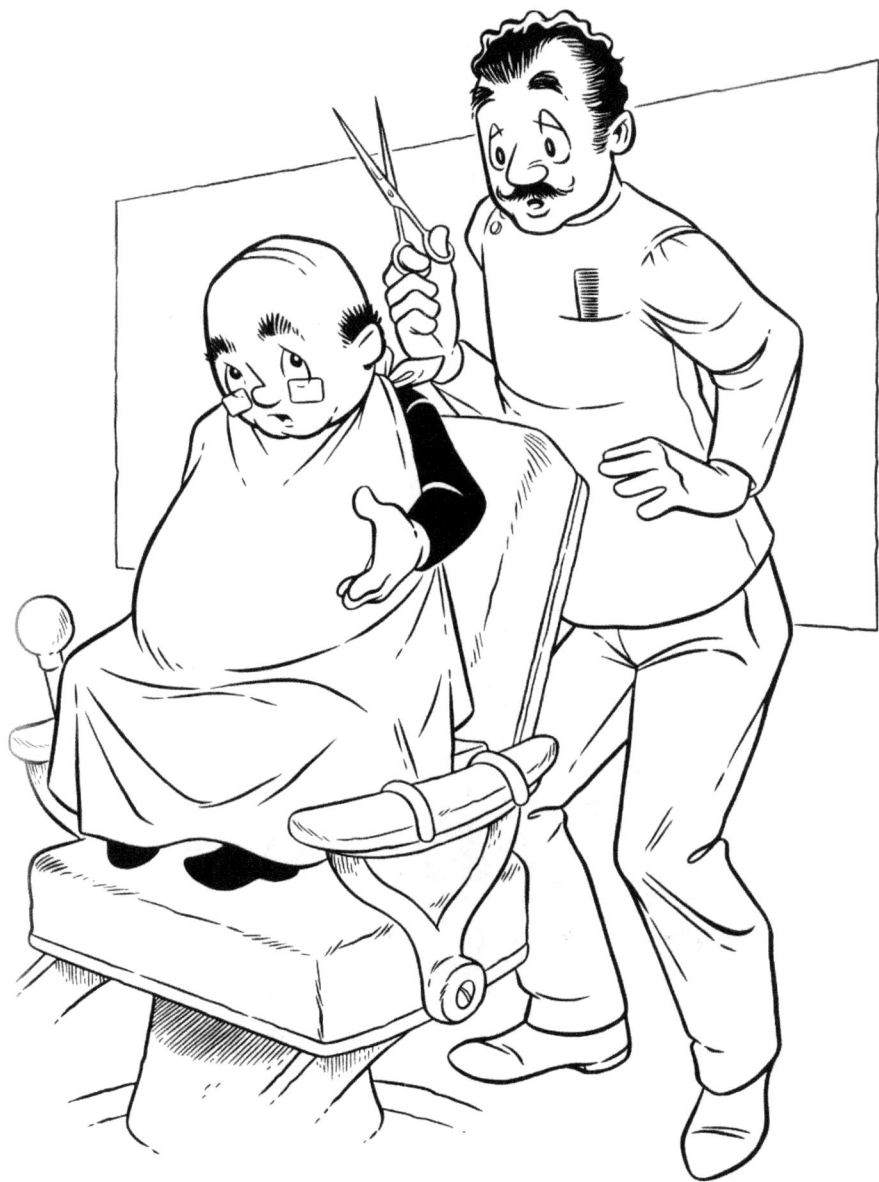

"YEP! TOMORROW I LEAVE FOR ROME—BY THE WAY, TONY, HOW DO YOU SAY 'CORNED BEEF AND CABBAGE' IN ITALIAN?"

"*Psst!* Have you seen today's *Daily Nun*??"

Little * Gabriel

Al Kilgore